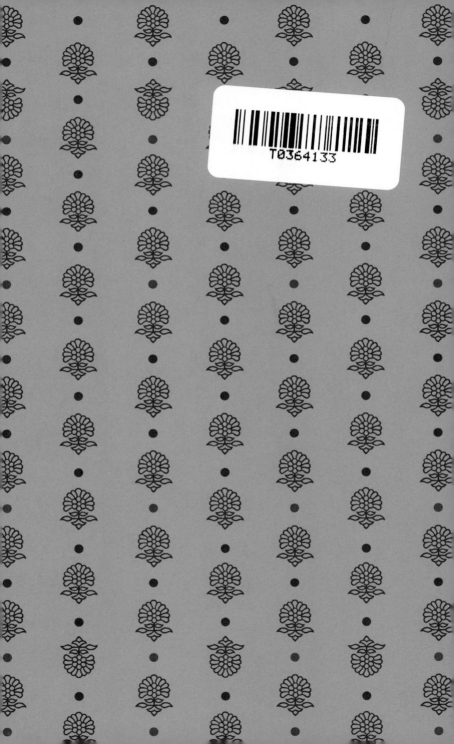

T0364133

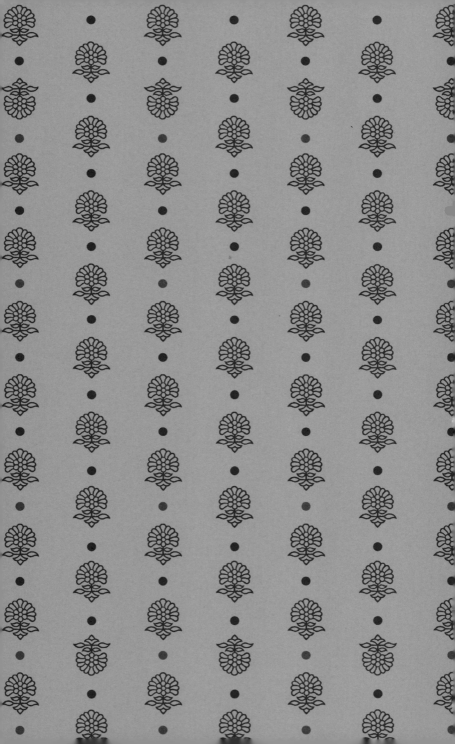

Things That Happen

. .

THE INDIA LIST

. .

Things That Happen
and Other Poems

BHASKAR CHAKRABARTI

• •

TRANSLATED BY ARUNAVA SINHA

CALCUTTA LONDON NEW YORK

• • •

Seagull Books, 2016

Originals © Basabi Chakraborty, 2016
English translations © Arunava Sinha, 2016

First published in English by Seagull Books, 2016

ISBN 978 0 8574 2 389 4

British Library Cataloguing-in-Publication Data
A catalogue record for this book is available from the British Library

Typeset and designed by Sunandini Banerjee, Seagull Books, Calcutta, India
Printed and bound by Hyam Enterprises, Calcutta, India

• • •

CONTENTS

• ∘ •

• •

All the world is made of poetry. On some days the doors and windows within are flung open. All that I see and hear, all that I get a sudden smell of, turns to something new in a moment. My body feels light. I have had glimpses of the astonishing world of poetry, and I have been astounded every time. So many wilting conversations, fragrances, glances and dreams are happily tacked up on its walls.

Why did I venture to write poetry? Life has surprised me exceedingly since childhood. As with everyone else, a lamp would burn constantly next to my existence, a magical glow. To a boy like me, from a poor family, indifferent to his studies, poetry came with the hope of freedom. If I could write great poetry—at eighteen or nineteen my notions were wide off the mark—I would get a good job. With a newspaper, at the very least. Not that poverty ever abandoned me. But what was remarkable was that my relationship with poetry had reached such a miraculous level of love that I never bothered much about employment or a steady job after this. For instance, I too had once been besotted by the idea of sky-high fame. But the past thirty or thirty-five years of my life have passed in such intense communion with poetry that I now feel there is something obscene about desiring fame.

I put aside sufficient time for writing new poetry. The preparations were made, but I have spent most of my life not writing poetry. If I do have some sort of history, it is the history of not-writing. It's not right to say I never had the time. Although I knew time was short, I honestly do not know even now why I did not write during all those hours that I could have written.

I am a poetryist. I love ordinariness. Rejected, pedestrian conversations and scenes, days and nights left behind are all things that move me. And I feel a desire to dress them in new clothes. Perhaps I wanted to capture an enormous pleasure in my poetry, the sound of very loud laughter. I did not succeed in keeping melancholy at a distance. But my poetry is not just mourning or city-centric or a delicious sauce. It's from the life I see around me, and the life I lead myself, that something like a folded paper boat surfaces. Perhaps my only task is to introduce this boat in different forms. Let the fact that I have felt a deeper form of love also be written down here.

Where does so much poetry come from? Is it only from a broken life and destroyed surroundings? What is the source of my themes? Who makes line after line of poetry float up in my mind like clouds? Who is it who dictates, 'Write this way,' or 'Write that way'? It's nobody but myself. The self I do not often encounter, the self I do not know much about, the self who stays with me round the clock and round the year, the self who goes everywhere with me, even goes to bed with me—that is the self which materializes when I write poetry. Which says, 'Sleep no more, open your eyes and see.'

Is poetry the language of silence? Does it seek the unknown amid the known? Is it the shadowy play of life and death? All right, I'll tell you what poetry is. It is a mountain with light on all its slopes, light that comes only from a thousand candles. The candles are all burning, and the mountain slowly unfurls its wings and floats away. This, to me, is poetry. Like a luminous mountain drifting away. I do not know very much more about poetry—this is the only image I see, that I *can* see. And I also feel that to perceive this beauty, existence must be turned into a tiny, weightless bird so that even when it is lost in the blue it can alight on the roof of your house in an instant. Poetry is as mysterious as space. No matter which age descends on earth, poetry will carve out its own path. Even when man travels in space one day, he will read poetry.

Possibly, poetry soothes my nerves. The tax we have to pay every day for survival is called loneliness. I have seen the most dangerous form of this loneliness. Poetry is becoming increasingly important in my life. Perhaps it is making living a little easier. I have never written poetry out of habit. Each of my books of poetry is my first book of poetry. From the very beginning my poetry has been open to taking any of two dozen or more different paths. Perhaps I am overstating the case about paths, but these days I feel the urge to wander off on each of them. I remember reading something beautiful once: 'The value of saying the right thing at the right time is one rupee, the value of being silent at the right time is two rupees.' I have always sought those two rupees when I wrote poetry.

I am indeed grateful to poetry. It is with poetry that I have taken the greatest liberties. I have ensured that empty optimism should never infiltrate my poetry. I must admit that I have never written political poetry. Still, if someone were to suddenly rush in and point at some of my poems and say, 'There, that's poetry, that's a political poem,' I wouldn't be particularly surprised. I am a night-time lover. Most of my poems are written at night. Night touches my insignificant poetry with its beautiful wings.

Writing poetry can be compared to constantly climbing a mountain with no summit. I have never considered writing poetry similar to buying a lottery ticket. I wanted poetry to wring me dry.

From the time I started writing poetry, I always felt that a poem can begin with any line, and end with any line too. Poetry must seem simple on the surface. It must have a thousand faces. And not discriminate between subjects. The distance between two lines of a poem must be at least one thousand kilometres. But in the invisible underbelly will lie the intimacy of millimetres.

Still exhaustion on me descends at times. Fatigue. Swiftness is lost. There are days when I lose my way, when I beat my head against a wall. When the world seems like a hospital in the afternoon. Why must the poetry of the past thirty or forty years from Bengal already seem like it belongs to the nineteenth century? Why must it appear to be nothing but a display of talent? Where has that intensity vanished, that feeling of being possessed? Even today there's a thing or two I wish to convey about poetry.

1. Poetry that resembles poetry or so-called poetry must be rejected.

2. Poetry must be released from all tyranny. It must be free. Traditional poetry must be stripped of its ornaments.

3. Words hold mysteries, they can be made into poetry.

4. All great poetry is simple, not all simple poetry is great.

5. After all kinds of poetry, an acute, new-fashioned poetry. A brand new world . . .

The Birds Are Chirping

One can stay away from poetry and people, it's a very difficult business. Times are such that we do not know how the neighbour survives, nor do we want to. Just a handful of poets in this world, whom we label nincompoops, are the only ones—I'll say this a hundred times—who are engrossed in dispelling this blindness and making the world a little more beautiful every day. We have seen countries splitting continuously, and poets rejoining the pieces.

When the truth had migrated from the beautiful into the light, and poetry from the village to the city, I was strolling on the banks of the Atreyee river in Balurghat one morning in the company of poets, writers and playwrights. A fragrance of purity had given me a gift of tranquillity. I was wondering whether to take a dip in the Atreyee when a writer friend suddenly told me that history would never forgive me. And would keep asking instead about the absence of nature in my poetry. How had nature lured me so sweetly into danger and then disappeared from my verses? When had I turned so ungrateful as to deny a place to the supplier of the plentiful milk that had nurtured me? Was that really the case? I can no longer remember.

If I was a night-time lover, how could I never have inserted even a slice of twilight in my poetry? Or the sunset? Or the vermilion? Still, I made one last attempt to defend myself. There's no nature, I said, but there are people. Humans. Standing at the terminus from where all the trains to hell departed, I used to savour the voices—of the bewildered, eccentric, dream-persecuted muttering man (I make the money, why should I not get my meals?), of the lover, of the lonely, abandoned woman whose wings are lost, of the middle-aged blonde woman in the kitchen who sang (moor your boat on my bank). All of them have entered my poetry. Effortlessly. Like nature.

—My years have not been kind to me. If history isn't either, what can one do?

I wrote a strange poem some twenty-six or twenty-seven years ago. Not that that's the point. But I took an intelligent decision—not to allow it to be published till now. I have an urge to pull this little poem out. In this context:

My Poetry

I have taken it with me to the market
Putting it in a basket like fruit
Looked at it alone from afar
It is exactly like me
My poetry

Why I Write

It's not just recently but for the past seven or eight years that the thought has kept confronting me: had I found a quiet, normal life instead of this one of writing poetry, I might have survived.

But, thinking it over, I've realized that sort of survival wouldn't have come easily to me. Under the impression that writing was the source of my anxiety and exhaustion, about seven years ago I gave it up for several months while in the throes of depression. I had thought of evicting this horrible poverty from my existence. I thought I would mingle with the crowds in this city of crowds and become one of them. I admit to a feeling of lightness at first. I felt fresh. The enormous expectation of fame from writing had vanished.

But no sooner had three or four months passed than a dart or two began to attack me constantly. The routine between home and the school, the school and home, and sleep, and cups of tea, and the newspaper made me gasp for breath. My jaws began to ache, everything tasted bitter. The pleasure dwindled. I began to coop myself up at home. In which case, why live any more? And as I was borne along on this stream of thought, the demon of 'must write' began to poke me again in the dead of night. To my great chagrin I discovered that I am what I am. Writing is my dharma. My existence. I have no choice but to write. And that's for survival too. The trouble begins when we ask for too much from life. It's the same with literature. 'Ask not for the outcome'—I'd read this and heard this so many times that it was possible to cling to this notion and resume writing.

I was given a tempestuous life, loaded with unbelievable vitality. Never mind luxuries—despite having the smallest of conveniences, I considered myself a street-dweller. There's a world that's unfamiliar and unknown to and unexplored by millions—I want to take it into another world. The thing is, there are many people for this task. So why did I have to be the one to jump at it? This is where I think the fundamental focus of my writing is concealed.

The scenes that my eyes continuously give birth to, the fascinating sounds and conversations that enter my ears and rock my world, the distant scents that make me wistful—no one can express these things of mine the way I can. Then who is going to write about these discarded, ordinary, overlooked matters? A lonely candle, a matchbox or two pairs of glasses embracing on a desk, a solitary young woman weeping in a moving taxi, the joy of girls leaning over the railing in a women's hostel—these fragmented scenes insinuate themselves into the folds of my mind and instigate me.

I write to glue my tattered perceptions together and make them float away on a breeze. I write to make our era roll, like a wheel, a little further beyond the sunset. The dreams, annoyances, alienation, medicines, pleasures, failures, laughter—all of these crowd my poetry. All I do is add a little compassion. I like to think that those who cannot see themselves even in the mirror will be able to recognize themselves accurately in my poetry.

I had wanted to graft new, living poems, in my own manner, on Bengali poetry. This is the desire I have always nurtured. But my perspective on writing has changed during different phases. Traversing death and reaching closer to life, friendship, human existence . . . I have often bent over a sheet of paper with a pen to take all of these to people.

I don't buy paper to write poetry, I buy it to spoil the white pages. I write for a tranquil, vigorous, brave new world. A world of joy. A joy that I want to reach out to and touch every day.

When Will Winter Come, Suparna?

(1971)

1967

That I'm still alive and active is a strange thought
According to Cheiro I should have died last year
But the breeze still plays on my body every day
I thought I'd write you a light-hearted letter about this
But I haven't managed to write the letter yet

I'd been to Captain Ghosh's house the other day
His daughter Rina played the harmonium and sang
   three songs for me
She goes to music school thrice a week,
   uses Keo Karpin oil
Reads some literature now and then, I was told
Captain Ghosh doesn't watch Bangla films at all

You should slow down when turning a corner in your car

The other day I met a man who hunts
We were standing on a wide terrace
Three gulps of vintage wine made him scream
My skin was dark earlier, do you know
The weather that makes tigers' pelts grow thick?

All year I wandered every lane and bylane in Calcutta

I even played some carrom, just like before
I haven't yet bought the books I meant to buy
There was commotion and a jackpot wherever I went
Screaming, shouting, and all round the year
So many foreign tourists came to Calcutta, schoolgirls
Dressed in identical clothes to sing the national anthem
Sixty-seven swelled in the wind
Your soundless mouth exploded everywhere

When Will Winter Come, Suparna?

When will winter come, Suparna, I'll sleep for three months—
    every evening
Someone plays a prank and transfers frog blood
Into my body, I sit in silence in the darkness
Some people set a blue balloon flying, there are fireworks
    all night
Celebrations, and then suddenly
All the candles go out together like magic, the festive day
Is blown away somewhere else like the wind, the whistles
Can no longer be heard, when I see water I want to plunge in
I feel an urge to submerge myself in it
And breathe with my head out of the water, I hate it, Suparna, I
Am not like humans, nor like light or dreams, my feet
Are growing broader all the time, the moment I hear
    the clatter of hooves
My heart trembles, I raise my face to breathe, I move the hands
Of the clock forward with my fingers, I hate it, when
Will winter come, Suparna, I'll sleep for three months
Once I saw, as soon as I woke at dawn, the clouds leaning
Near the window, darkness everywhere
I couldn't even see my own nails clearly that day
Weeping when I remembered you, I took a match to my head,
Falling asleep again to the smell of burning hair

I am no longer human now, walking down the road, I
Feel the urge to leap suddenly, I no longer like sitting
Submissively before love for a long three months, whenever
I hear human footsteps
My breath turns ragged, I run away in the direction I came from
Why do I run? I hate it
When will winter come, Suparna, I'll sleep for three months

The Beggar (*1 / 37*)

The skin on his face is taut, people say,
  'A serious man, lives alone in a corner'
Serious about what? Oh, just because I write a poem or two?
You know, fuck it, that I'm a bigger beggar than beggars
Taking my shoes off at the bottom of the stairs
I climb up to your secluded room, climb down—in-between, you
Talk of the tea market, of where there has been extra rain
  this year
Some days you smile, raise your eyebrows, and say, 'Oh it's you!
  Come on in.
Been so long, not since the twenty-seventh.'
I see that, even more than nourishing you,
Bournvita has made you garrulous

And yet a swan flutters in my breast whenever I see a telephone
  at nine in the morning
Like baby goats the sunlight frolics on the parapet
Will everything fall to earth?
Just the one birth—I run up, you know I *will* run
I *will* sit cross-legged where your shadow falls
I am brick, I am wood—I am lime and sand or a toothpick
You know, fuck it, that I'm a bigger beggar than beggars
Even today, smiling like a fool,

I climb up to your secluded room, climb down—people say,
'A serious man, lives alone in a corner'

The Ox

I crouch near your horns, not knowing when the moon
Rises, when the clouds
Shroud us both, you and me
Sand flies everywhere, in the darkness the shadow cast by
  your body
Grows longer
Wisps of straw trail near your curved horns, the stomach swells
Somewhere a plump crow caws and flies away, as if
They've walked miles, clerks come home, light the lamp, kiss
Their wives and go to bed
Somewhere lightning flashes in some people's eyes, at night
Do they let their hair loose, part their legs and sob? How
The years pass, years and years, I
Crouch near your horns, not knowing when the moon
Rises, when the clouds
Shroud us both, you and me

Winter

Your hair is flying in the wind, you're holding your phone
  in your left hand
I have returned again to your room by winter light
Your cat, I notice, is not
As swift as before, your ball of wool
I see, is rolling away, rolling further beneath the slanting bed
I'm sitting in silence, your cat is yawning in silence
The winter waterfall is receding after· calling out to us in vain

My Little Sister

Should I watch over her
When my little sister sleeps

The sky turns blue in the afternoon
The silent tumult of the body

Should I sleep by her side
When my little sister sleeps

Remnant

Like a narrow lane, a long corridor
Only a chair will remain in the corridor all night tonight

From the bushes
The moon will leap up
From the corner of the stairs the cat will shift towards the stove
   tonight

Only a pin will remain swaying in the wind all night tonight
Only a man will remain standing on the unprotected roof all
   night tonight

About Silence

That was what my life was like, I would wander deep
Into the heart of unfamiliar homes

I bend over your old letter tonight
The roads of Egypt are now
Distant from us, once, we had wanted to walk on them
Do you remember? Do you?

About silence, I can, if you like, write some more
To inform you, look at me now
Look how I'm walking downstairs to the kitchen now
Gurupada next door has long fallen asleep
The mousetrap is in pursuit of the mouse

Burnt charcoal sparkles on both sides of the floor

The Camel

I'm your companion too—travelling across the sand all my life
Supple neck, dull eyes that see no celebrations
Listen, I have
Stayed up many night—like a fool, written much poetry
Do you have a manager?
I will give more, cactus, I will cash in my coin—or in the
    afternoon
I will peep into the restaurant kitchen
You and I have a fever in the evening
Look, Jhumpa and Jhumpa's mother are sitting alone in
    the veranda
Spring is here—let's go—take me to your land

Come, Good News, Come

(1981)

After Tossing and Turning

I'm very uncomfortable when I consider that I know nothing about dogs. There are so many dogs of different colours and shapes and size in this world, all extraordinary. Pomeranians. Terriers. Wherever I go I hear tales of dogs. Dogs that talk like humans, dogs that lie quietly on beds like humans. When the summer days arrive, I clap and bathe several times and listen to stories about dogs. At some point the drink is drained from the glass. At some point the roads are drained of people on the way back in the tram or the bus. As I return home, I think only of dogs. Lying in bed, my love, all that remains is tears and tossing and turning. Tagore's birthday comes, we shave with fresh blades again.

To William

William, William, can you hear me? I can't keep the window open against the wind this morning. On this stormy day in Calcutta I'm seeking you, I want you near me, when the eternal heart-breaking song of the earth is playing all day and all night beneath the clouds—when the wind is whistling through the gooseberry leaves, and I'm trembling in terror every now and then. Can you hear me, William? Are you turning over on your side? Fear is hammering away at me today. I can see the devil salivating constantly—I see the barrel of the gun approaching me calmly. I want you to turn up in the rainstorm. To get out of that mysterious blue taxi. Come, and sit on this chair by my side—I want us to spend time together again.

The Hammer

. . .

I know the hammer will come rushing one day and smash my head. For thousands of years I have been waiting, and so has that silent, solid hammer. Will it be on a winter day? Or a spring night? I wonder. I can see you. I kiss you. When I'm moving about I see you moving about too. When I'm hanging, I see you hanging too, not far from the balcony. I like it that you don't wear clothes, that you lie down on the stairs, in the hospital, that you stand next to me when I'm alone on the street. I went to the doctor and told him about you. I went to a woman and told her about you. When winter descends on Calcutta next, I'll no longer pull the quilt over my head. I will watch, I'll keep watching, you advancing towards me. I will say, I salute you, my lord, I salute you.

Blood

Now friends' faces
Can be seen far away
From a table to my table
Fake laughter and tears, loathing
Concealed rage
Waft into my room
I can see
I can hear

Here it rains all day now
There
Friends flanking friends
Letters in their breast pockets
Full of superfluous
Reassurance. A dagger, just
Gouging holes. I look up
To see friends put some currency on the table
And leave in twos and threes
Friends, in twos and threes
Fall asleep at the table, walk
From far away I too begin my lonely walk
Blood drips
Blood drips and falls

Come, Good News, Come

The days, just like wheels
Without reason
Grind me

—Getting off the bus I felt
I was still aboard. Yet
Who's that girl?

She looks
Like someone from home
Minu's sister, perhaps. Come
Good news, come—
I have no other wish
Just let that girl
Marry
Our young poet

All I Have

I only know of poverty
I know of nothing else

I have seen the girl with a face of sorrow
I have seen nothing else

I only understand
Matters of love
I understand nothing else

In Thirty-Two Years

I see you often in an unknown land
Standing on a derelict roof

Nothing
More to say

No words, no dreams
Only some days and nights remain

Daal

When the daal refuses to be cooked
The entire house
Is sullen. After his bath
My father waits. After her bath
My sister waits.
And in the morning, I am startled
The entire house is quiet
My mother sits by the stove

Memory

Oh it's still so familiar
The sound of the night train

I rise
And get back down to bed

I close my eyes, it floats up
Still we sit in silence face to face

Tears arrive

In the Restaurant

I'm sitting near the language-lover
Now the afternoon passes, slowly, it leaves

I remember embraces
I remember calm, smiling faces

There's poison in my blood, my darling
Now life passes, slowly, it leaves

On the Streets Once More

(1983)

Poem 129

I have no favourite writer. I
Read a book, and then shut
The book. I run, leap
Into bed. Ah.
The bed is my friend for ever
My peace, consolation, life's reward
So many books on the shelves, so many writers
But where's the writer
Oh, where,
Whose characters only lie in bed?

A Letter

Therefore I'm starting with therefore
There's not much to write
Ganesh has run away. So
The house is again as dirty as before
One of the windowpanes has broken
I had thought of dressing the new days
In colourful, brand-new clothes
If I came into some money, I thought
We could move in together now
I have no stamps
So I'm sending this letter by hand
Forgive me

Poem 137

Waking up this morning I thought of myself, without warning,
As Jesus Christ. I
Ran to the mirror, I found
My face covered in a beard, my eyes beautifully open, who is
The tailor who made these clothes for me?
For two hours I sat silently in the room
For two hours I paced silently in the room
Mother Mary gave me a cup of tea and a biscuit
In the evening, when it was dark everywhere, I saw in surprise
There was blood on my hands, blood on my feet, my friends,
    my brothers
What is this room you have borne me into?
A fat and dark doctor plunged an unnecessary needle into me

Poem 143

My time is done. And with it, my life.
There's nothing much to regret any more.
Although a couple of small tasks are incomplete
Such as reassuring the terrified boy who lives
Down the road, 'There's nothing to fear.'
Such as writing a letter to a new friend,
'Pay a visit one day to the haunted house.'

Brothers Mine (1/107)

I had written of barbed wire
It seems someone has eaten it all up
I had written of a broken-down ship
It seems someone's hidden it in their pocket
Days of wandering around the city, days of seeing paintings
My day to stand quietly in the street with my hands
  in my pockets
All of you must come back to me
I want to show you again where the poison has been hidden
I want to inform you once more that the dazzling days
  rushing towards us
Are only for our children
Who whine for ice cream and hide behind their mothers' saris
Look, like a xylophone the newlyweds walk along the street
Look, a stamp, a tiger worth fifteen paise
Night after night, for countless years, I've wanted to slice myself
  open for self-examination
I have swallowed alcohol with ashes in it
I have gone up to fallen women to tell them, 'I love you.'
Not all of this was a game.
My blood and sweat are mingled with black and white days,
  brothers mine
I have forgotten nothing, none of it

The blows and the humiliation and the tears
Look—it's so late tonight as well—still I cannot sleep.

Contrition

Before you leave, evening,
Tell me something

Even today I
Want to live, even today
I see, when I'm about to
Laugh brightly without warning

That my expression is still
As glum as Hooghly District

On the Streets Once More

Green wooden veranda, you
Have taught me
To be alone. Alone I wear
Myself down roaming run-down streets
Once more. Again
The sweaty days came
The summer storm came. I saw
Many new things.
A photograph of a tiger in a bookshop
Its mouth open, its roar
Inaudible
I heard that Sumanta has again
Left his wife and run away yesterday

The Giuoco Piano

I've been playing chess against myself since evening
Both the queens are mine
Four rooks, four bishops, all of them
Following my commands. What time is it now?
Did anyone come looking for me?
I cannot control my two queens at night any more
When dawn breaks
I'm thinking of walking far, far away
After which I'll consider whether to come back home
      ever again

A Prayer: 2

Come, dark clouds
Cleanse this civilization

Everywhere there's just
Arid politeness
Now let the dry smiles
Stop. Come.

Let people sit in their own rooms
And weep again.

A Distant Table

I'm getting old. Why talk of kingfishers?

Me, I liked handloom saris very much
In the nineteen sixties

I liked the woman in the handloom sari even more

That was many years ago
A little tired now, but still I like seeing

Four or five people sitting around a woman
At a distant table

Goodbye

A shadow. What shadow is this
Life has slowed down to a stop

Beside whom do you lie down, night
Who is it whose bed you make today

I walk
All I do is walk

Goodbye, playroom where I played

With the Lord
(1986)

1

On a whim this afternoon I went to the city on a minibus
    with the lord
For a few minutes we sat face to face in a restaurant, laughing
A girl in an embroidered sari sat at our table and left at once
'I love girls very much,' I said—my lord
Smiled, scribbled something quickly, then
Disappeared, leaving me in the crowd
If the girl calls me to her I won't go looking for the lord today
If the girl calls me to her I won't go home alone today

2

The lord has left me and taken the evening train to Dehra Dun
I live by myself in a small room, so the light does not
Illuminate my body, or mind. I too want to leave the suburbs,
Leave this shattered city for the mountains or the sea breeze
The lord heard me out with a cigar in his hand and laughed
'Although you are not the sheriff,' he said, 'you must tend
To this devastated metropolis.' I'm told my responsibilities are
    immense
I want to merge into every water body, but the lord is unwilling
And has disappeared again—I lie quietly in an even-emptier
    room

3

It's been two or three days since I met the lord or got a telegram
Distress, like a giant bird, flutters its wings against my face
Walking all by myself through the lane I imagine
With half a glass of tea in the spring afternoon I imagine
I'm still walking along the street so easily with that girl
And we're rinsing our faces in a joyous breeze that blows
Perhaps I will never glimpse the lord again, I also know
The handloom sari will never appear by the scrapped iron
On the broken-down road, but we're still in touch
Not being in touch is ungodly, so I write letters even today

4

I met the lord quite easily once again this evening
I found that the lord is connected to bathing
I lie in calmness, my glasses have come off
The lord presents a case on happiness to me
The sounds of cars and construction are wafting in
A couple of somewhat loud young men are returning
Not a candle or a sister at home, nor money in the pocket
Still the heart can reach the breeze and people—a rainswept face

5

Our conversations began, Lord, in nineteen eighty-two
'Bhaskar isn't modern,' let them write this next year
I want to hear a couple of things in private, Lord mine
I'm writing since the morning, I'm opposed to going to work
Peace has descended like light since this morning

Today the wind has dropped from the sky without effort
How intimate this connection in my commonplace room
Children's laughter has covered this house—the station road

6

No car ever enters the lane where I live, Lord
You'd better walk alone, barefoot, to my house
We'll spread a sheet on the roof and talk some more at night
I've told you the subject already, lower-middle-class problems
Bring some cigarettes, bring matches and history books
I want to show you life stories from towns and bazaars and villages
Lit up on the silent Ganga currents, what is this boat whose
Light floats further away? Even today I watch from a distance

7

At last the sky has risen, Lord, in the room
Such clear photographs, what camera is this?
Familiar faces all, thin, torn, plagued by anxiety
Worrying is the electrified curse of this century
Lord, I draw your face in my notebook
What daily destitution is this that's touched me
Perhaps I have glimpsed a road today on which
A simple traveller walks, a simple light burns

8

At least I have somewhere to take shelter
Slums are destroyed, tall buildings grow taller

I don't seek your company like a beggar, you know
In this empty house I can live in greater loneliness
I want to sleep, my Lord, a sad slumber overwhelms me
The wilted faces seem to droop even more
You never told me to walk the streets alone. Why?
Just a couple of nights, I remember, sleeping on the road

9

You are zero-zero-seven, O Lord, you are always nearby
But keep your eye on me today, you must have earned
Your martial-arts black belt—look, there's the enemy eleven
Poverty, anxiety, alienation, loneliness—look—
Have surrounded me at home, on the street, in cafes
I want to sing songs just songs in my life just songs
The flag, of love, has long slipped out of man's grasp
Leaping, somersaulting
Can you bring me that banner? Let me test your skills

10

Did you send the breeze for me this April night?
But I've quietened down already, still we met again,
This time, after a long hiatus, like Dolly's smile,
This wind of peace is pleasing, I have forgotten
Everything from my scorched life, forgotten
What I said, the streets I walked. I climbed
Onto the roof at midnight to understand the language
Of your eyes, the meaning and light. This night is not wasted

11

You touched me and so I'm serene like marble
Where on earth were you
So many days and nights lost in futile labour
Anyhow, because you are here now joy has come
People have come, they
Place their hands on my heart and happily sing and talk
I want to bring them peace, to wipe out
Their anxieties, I want to give them gifts
Of laughter and sleep and intimacy, this ordinary life of mine

12

Perhaps you were abroad, so I couldn't sleep last night
Were you sitting quietly by the sea or on a mountain?
Maybe you were busy giving autographs with a smile
To children in this enormous city
I was in serious trouble last night, you know
Every time I closed my eyes that first girl's face swam up
You tell me, we have children now
Is it right for her face to swim up?
This was how all of last night passed. This afternoon—
I don't remember the book that I was reading—
I'm telling you now, listen
Wherever you may be, send your address, I want to write a letter

13

You are a young boy, Lord, I'm going to put a young girl
In charge of looking after you and slip away somewhere far

I'll go to Benaras, I'll go to an unknown forest
Not to hunt, but to reel in drunkenness
I shall float from leaves on trees to leaves on trees
Like the water I shall only whirl in water
I have no regrets because you neglect me
I think the young girl will look after you better

14

Not one but two world wars in our century—it makes me worry
So the next war will start two years from now?
I live in terror, I live in shame, my Lord
This is a terrible war, humiliating to mankind
Why can't you fly across the world like a white dove?
Go perch on the shoulders of Russia and of America
Be my friend and explain to them, save the world's children
A strange century, this is the darkest time, we're tainted today

15

Unfurl your wings with besotted eyes, let me see you expand
Let us listen to your music, I only want to paint
I have no camera, you know I do not want your photograph
I do not want discussions on the theory of illumination
Just a wistful anklet on your feet. I'm in the garden today
The cafe was where I lived once, I've shed those clothes
I knew the mother sent her drug-addict son 125 every month
The wall that rises will be demolished one day
And the ancient world will be new, I know this
Today, show me your dance

Heart, touch the lord with the thousandth hand
Look, a flash, wings, black clouds gathered beneath the sky

16

It's a lot like running from the battlefield to your window
I'll tell you all in the course of conversation, but remember
There is no need to nurse me, the glory of the sky floats up
I sweep away exhaustion
Smoking, I note down that we met on the second day
Of Shrabon
I have recorded your loud and innocent laughter on a cassette
Shall I pass my days like a fool then? I have no money
No, never mind. This light, I realize, dispels the dark
In your drawing room or at tea we will meet again some evening

17

If not to talk to you, why do I sit alone on the roof at night?
Such strange days and nights with no flesh on their bones
A thousand skeletons have surrounded me now
But still I long to return to the remote village
For that girl who just became a woman
I yearn to sink into an unknown lane
To sail to Nigeria
I want to tell you all this, have you nothing to say?

18

I forget you again, the days are a failure, the nights too
All of life seems the middle of the afternoon

Travelling alone in a mysterious train compartment, I see
The village bride—her sari's flying in the wind
Is that where you are?
Are you in the tumult of the naked boys cavorting
By the rail tracks? Are you their leader? Listen
These days I can walk calmly and with ease
Matching steps with your famous friend, Death

19

You, young man, are complicated, which is why you are
In the wind and on the road, you're the lamp on the desk
In your yellow shirt you seem a glib wordsmith at the cafe
How often will you betray me, I'm buying a ticket, let me tell you
I know we'll meet again in the sound of rain on a local train
A well-wisher will make me buy infinite incense and intimate combs
Do you have nothing else to do? Then let me go
Nearer more people, I love them, call the girls

20

I have found my No.1 friend—he has no other friends
We keep talking easily
All the time, sometimes we fall silent, our words calm
We make no pretence of protocol or socializing
We have no telephones
But still I want to traffic from continent to continent
This green and intense word 'friendship'
The address is at the bottom left, confidential communication
    is possible
But before nine in the morning or in the evening

21

I'm off again, there is no destination, only a signal

Every time I shut my eyes, is that a mahout riding a huge elephant

Or is it you? Then show me the way

I cannot bear this living like a ghost

Why did you not give me a mask?

Why didn't you cover me in the caress of a wig?

You know the smell of my soul, innocent heart

I rose at dawn today

The wind is whiter today, I'm drifting even more today towards you

22

Whatever pride I had you swept away, I have become simpler

Today I am humble, free

I move among easy-minded people, without a trace of sadness

I float, I drift, like a feather in the breeze, listen,

I have tossed off all my coloured clothes, in this mystery light

I smelt the sea on the breath of sailors, I am not

Enough of a lover, but still I understand

That this is a wondrous love, the question marks have vanished

23

The clouds are lower in the evening, are you sitting by my
 window, lord?

I have been wounded again, I inhale nicotine day and night

Tobacco has only made me feeble and bankrupt

I no longer get any joy from road trips, you know

You have given up my company, and yet and yet and yet

 I'm not despondent

I still fall into dark holes, I warn my friends
One day they will touch the days of joy
Sitting by the ancient fort
I too will do my work, and then wipe out this name before I go

24

If you and I went to Baroda and stayed back
We might enjoy ourselves this time
For so long now there's been no fun, no playing
For a long time I've been sitting in this trouble-free
House. My friend of light
Why go to Barisha or Jadavpur in Calcutta? Let's go to Baroda
And swim in the wind—like topsy-turvy people
Let's leap in green fields
Let's lie down, compose a song of deep and intense love

25

Who do you think you are to infest my life again and again?
I live on daily wages, I'm not a member of extreme society
You can go to Mr Acharya's house and bless his children
So that they pass the exams and find beautiful livelihoods
Let my days pass as they pass now
Let my penniless longings drown in the water if they must
Still I will note down dreams of fawns and dreams of trees
I'll go to Bethuadahari with the girl, don't annoy me any more.

The Sky Will Be Partly Cloudy
(1989)

To Lorca

A teardrop fell in the desert
My mother and younger sister went looking

With cotton swabs and medicine
The doctor arrived
In a black robe, the lawyer came

Like a man without a tongue I remained silent
For a full three months
Then I reattached my wings to my body one day

And began flying

To Sing and Dance

I am bound to write about every bend in the road
I am compelled to write about Mrs Mathew, meaning
I'm burning too though a smile dangles from my lips
Be well, mothers mine
Beneath the stairs and in the hospital, be well
Adorn the night with flowers and leaves

Come, girls, come with me
I want to write about your silken hair
Your glowing cheeks, your twinkling eyes make me joyful
    even today
What a wasted, misguided childhood I have spent
I've been flung into the desert today, my poetry has no balcony
    to stand on

I am bound to write of the river in my head
I write about
The looming danger and its stench
I write of the woodpecker and the faded wicker chair
The afternoon beckons me today like a cock's crest
Come, girls, let's go together
The fog has gathered, come, let's get ready to sing and dance

Wings

I float on the breeze
From your eyes and mouth

Perhaps I'd forgotten
There was fear, there was the city of anxiety

Today the windows are open
Today, in the room,

Two simple, becalmed lilies

Are scattered

The Chair of Time

That was early one morning
When, opening the windows
My eyes saw only light
The beauty of a world without wars
Dropping on a serene earth

The newspaper is stilled in the hand
Why do you have no words today?
Is the knife beneath the white table
Flashing in the darkness of the light?

I was borne in on the high tide
I shall go back on the ebbing waters
Between these two, I watch mutely
The decade coming with promises
Breaking its promises, and leaving

Buddha

The light in your eyes tells me to be tranquil
I write about you this twenty-first of July, Buddha
These complications, this city, flames, disguises
This pretence of love, ceasefire, hypocrisy
Push me to a distance, where your visage tells me
Be more tranquil—live like the sunlight in winter

Epitaph

Between two sighs, Death,
I saw you being born

Memories: 3

The face from twenty-five years ago
Is like a Japanese ideogram

Armlet twinkling softly
Music, music, just music

Lying in a tiny room today
I remember being a lover once

. • .

Rehearsals for Dreaming

(1993)

Tangles

A life of mistakes like a ghost a death of mistakes like a ghost is
   toying with me
What's the date today is it Monday or Tuesday I'm trying to
   find out and I just can't remember just can't
The sweet and broken and crumpled faces are hovering over
   the streets now
I can see why melancholy sank its teeth into me at nineteen and
my head is beginning to hang with shame
What's the date today my breath is still circulating in our
   suburbs although this room is tiny now and the days are
   damaged and the nights have no cracks
Full of happiness a fresh young woman's face of sixty-two or
   sixty-three so many smiles smiling in silence and glasses and
   writing her self-satisfied diary
Where did the explosion take place melancholy I let you mingle
   with my blood when I was just nineteen
A narrow boat sailed past every afternoon where were my eyes
   where my education when on the frozen table electric shocks
   devoured my mind
Careful death a dangerous gentleman brought a telegram
My head is beginning to hang with shame
Am I forgetting my burnt orange dreams I cannot remember I
   am racing down B. T. Road my teacher is saying I mustn't pause
   for breath when reciting declensions

Why can't I wander around at night a learned and ancient
   philosopher was born today in the torrential rain
Full of happiness a fresh young woman's face so many smiles
   smiling in silence and glasses and hands in repose
On a summer morning through a bus window our city our
   Calcutta keeps drifting keeps drifting
Someone said who was it who said the rain will be on the next
   tram I cannot remember I cannot remember all day and all
   night my nerves whisper
When fingers keep groping for a relationship in the empty
   postbox
When I observe as I lie in the belly of a gigantic python
My funeral procession moving towards the crematorium slowly
   while I follow.

The Horse

At the bottom of the stairs is a horse from nowhere with
   shattered knees
I don't know if he loves his master
What if he gets into a frenzy some day, I fret

It could easily happen
Perhaps he will rub his face roughly on the cement one day
No grass here, no companions
Who brought this creature here?
Do horses suffer from depression of any kind?
Or anxiety?

Mr Nerve was calm and cooperative that evening
As I went quietly down the stairs from the terrace
But once I entered my sleep-white bed
Who could claim it was peaceful? At the bottom of the stairs

Such an outburst of music, such loud conversation!
You there, pass the easy chair this way
Are you asleep? You there!

In the Floating Darkness

On my way back darkness had settled comfortably over the
　　narrow lane
Not all faces have become masks yet, I was thinking to myself
And I might even remember a snatch from a song

Last night's dream had a white feather or two. A couple of
　　blue feathers.

A moss-covered building.
Parimal-babu lived with his family two houses away.
That one was almost moss too.

The leaves that I raked my nails across
The yards on the horizon I had agitated in
The eyelids I had planted kisses on

Were not grenades. Nor the hunters' caps they wear these days.

A Minute's Silence

The sky is a trifle red. Nothing serious. Just another extra person
Among Calcutta's millions
Is lost, he's been lost

I wonder what the matter with him was. Any idea?
It's a strange tale
All he did through the day was make a colourful coffin

I notice the evening sky is often red. Nothing serious.
A lanky man
Whom neighbours knew nothing about
A light would burn in his room at dead of night

I wonder what he did

Must have been reckless

In a lane a blue bird abandoned the sky and vanished
Just vanished without a trace

Things That Happen

The days aren't passing badly for the two of us
Though it's true we haven't been to the hills,
We haven't been to the seaside, for three years now
And poverty, it's no small annoyance
Constantly borrowing money and asking my sister for help
Still, one or two interesting things do happen
Tonight, for instance, you exclaimed: There, it's raining
We went up to the window
But it was only the sound of someone pissing on the roof
   next door
Or the other night, I was writing in the tiny room
With the light on—someone from the street said loudly
Go to sleep, motherfucker

The Face

Not a trace of blood on the face, but still
How bloody the face is.

A thousand horns are here——thousands all around
Have you, for me, entered this city today, river?

Sometimes I stow away this silent face on the table
Sometimes a boat in a dream that I put this face in

Today, though
On this wingless April afternoon
Placing this faceless face next to yours I imagine

This face will sleep again at night one day——one day
It will regain its glory

In the Tricoloured Light

Whirling in the wind, a face or two falls to the ground
How horrifying, how irksome the sound is
It seems to have a connection with my life somewhere

Will the quarrels and cursing in the common bathroom
  and swearing
Next door ever end?
An annoyance, a sadness today, as tall as
An eleventwelvefifteen-storeyed building
To tell the truth I know nothing at all about Putu Chowdhury
In the tricoloured light
The other day on the pavement I was reading a memorial plaque
'Smoking prohibited' and I had gone and lit a cigarette.

Humans are a type of tree, my dear sir, that can walk
I dream of a trouble-free world, Professor,
That will perhaps never materialize

But, tell me, why should it not?

Freeze Frame

A tree and
Beneath the tree a hemp-and-bamboo cot
Our third world

Touch

Just
To talk to the night I came up to the terrace tonight
Love has promised all my senses have promised
They will return to us one day
Tonight I do not want to hear a loud blowing of the nose renting
   the skies
Or the owl's historic hooting
O Night, O deepening Night, petrol night, Malkosh night
Let the transplanted kidneys start working now
Let these faces drop silently into my life
It's true we have ruined our lungs ourselves and sleep and
Our lives
The man who delivered a weighty lecture the other day is
Of no concern to us
Income tax is no concern to us either
Why should we stuff a cartridge
Into our left brain or right
All of us are innocent criminals
Some people suddenly turn into windows and we can see
Life without distortion
The woman by my side has named me 'The Wall', however, and
For several years I have been standing mutely
Still, fruit grow as beautiful as fruit one day

Laughter hovers all around
We name the room 'care room', we name the room 'plenitude'
Even before dawn I shall barge into the narrow tea shop today
I'll hear the boys swapping fishing tales
I'll hear: 'Don't leave me don't leave don't . . . '
Just this joy
Only for this joy will I move black death further by an inch today
I will keep gazing at this dawn of mine today at dawn

Narrow Lanes

This year
I will finally have seen
All the narrow lanes in the world

On some afternoons and evenings
Friends'
All the dead friends' faces come back to me

No body within, whose shirt, whose shirt is that hanging in
  the balcony

At the doctor's chamber tears in a decent woman's eyes
And an unknown young man
Testing the brakes of his new motorbike

(Who knows where they're going)

I have not yet met the horizon my love

All I see are unspeaking lights shrouded in mist
Narrow lanes
The city's seashell belches

The Crime

This morning I did nothing I only parted the window curtains
Slightly
Nothing important nothing historic nothing revolutionary,
None of these, I just parted the window curtains
Slightly this morning.
Do I have the right to part the curtains?
The right to view the suburbs through the window
—You could have gone back to bed after your tea and the toilet
—Yes I could have but this morning I parted the window curtains
Slightly
The voices are scattering slowly in different directions
I shall be executed today, though I don't know the exact time

The Memory of Golden Hair

My mother would say, I know why
You don't stay home. On torrid afternoons
We'd both lie on the floor. My relationship
With the river that flowed next to the house
Had become sluggish
It was, possibly, a blue song that
Would make me leave home, with hardly
Any money for the road, I
Would float from one part of the city to another
An afternoon with half a cup of coffee
Fragments of hoarse voices in the evening
These days I wonder where
The wind comes from and where it goes. Who knows where
In her sari with the wide red border, my mother
Is muttering to herself now
In my head a dreadful typhoon is knotting itself up again
Will I ever be able to disclose everything?

Sleep

The babies are falling asleep. Stop
Your babbling. Sleep.

The rivers seek rest
They're folding their wings at dusk

I have lost mine
Today sleep
Has claimed my eyes too

Absence

There will be no sharp sound
Not a single teardrop will roll anywhere
Maybe someone will say, 'Good riddance.'
Perhaps someone will write, the beanpole's gone
I will make friends with a new giraffe
I will become acquainted with Platero's nephew
While we're looking at our world from a distance
Maybe you will be
Returning home with a couple of oranges or pears you bought
A strange night-like feeling everywhere
Possibly loud speeches are still being made by the road
Think about it, gentlemen

The White Paper Bird

A white paper bird is beating its wings on this blind night

I've noticed for the past few days
You have been trying to sweep out of your yard
All that is old, all that is dead
All that is rotten, all that is stinking

Those who went to live on the moon
Are dying to return to earth now

Your anxiety your fear your insomnia are a lot like rubber
Your three children are waving at you from a distance in the mist
Another cigarette now, at midnight?
You'll never amount to anything
Pour yourself a glass of chilled water, go to bed

Send a new letter or two silently into the void through the window

You Are My Sleep

(1998)

Manik

The trees have taken the day off
We won't be talking today

My friends are all
Busy with their children's weddings
Busy with their novels
Busy with their films

There, like a decent sort
Like a polite man I said: Friends
Was I right?
Do I have any friends any more?

Just the other day I wrote to one of them
'I think of you quite often.'
Who talks like that in '96?
Whatever happened at twenty-one or twenty-two
Is best forgotten now.

Now I am reminded of a ship sometimes
I recollect a mast
I might have actually told Manik about this
But Manik has been gone a long time

The Horse

I forgot to write to you that
The horse has plunged from the second floor
On the cement
And in fact
Has been shattered into seven or eight pieces
This isn't
Important, though, what is
Is my writing
Banerjee-babu is on holiday
I'm writing to you, the horse could
Actually have a conversation
In a room made of air
One day he sang a song
Lovely. I was in bed
I stayed in bed
When I looked in astonishment
At the horse, I heard:
This isn't anything special
Things like these do happen sometimes

Muralidhar

1

Does the world taste bitter to you too, Muralidhar?
What would you have done if you had a pair of wings?
I don't think, personally, men wish to fly any more
At most, they go in search of another cup of tea
They scribble a letter or two, or they escort
Their brother's wife all the way to Ranaghat
No longer, Muralidhar, can I get into crowded buses
Nor can I stay up nights like I used to
Did you manage to complete your memoir?
Our days will become bearable when you return
We will become indefatigable again
But when are you coming back, Muralidhar? When?

2

Murlidhar, I'm forced to think of you some more
Where are you? And what is it you're up to?
We have all but died and become spirits
I had hoped to see the ship's arrival announced
One of these days and feel euphoric
The love that we had imagined

Has remained beyond our reach, after all
Everyone's forgotten you. You should know
No one's talked of you in a long while.
I, who grew up on the streets, next to a slum
Play anywhere I like now, I listen to speeches
Why do people deliver so many lectures?
I can't write or anything. I have no wings.
Should I give up, Muralidhar? Or should I leave?

Journey

Come, let's stand on the street. We'll talk on the footpath.
The street is desolate today. There's no breeze.
Three hundred talents whispering in the room. Are you
Under the impression that poetry is a matter of three
Or three and a half minutes? A journey consumed by eyes
Today. A journey started such a long time ago.
A 'no' from such a long time ago has appeared
I have pushed death away from the table. I must
Keep my brain free. I must sing. Where has all the
Music gone? I am not
A lump of superstitions. Not a misogynist.
I want to stand on the street and talk. Come
Let's stand on the footpath. We'll talk. Converse.
The day the leaves are shed
The day the leaves drift to the ground, it seems
Life holds nothing more. A journey through
Destitution, as it were. A slowness.
And the days the roads turn dark
And fat raindrops batter the body
What can we do
What is there for us to, besides consoling
All that lamentation, with its bundles, a little?

Panskura

Trouble is, words elude me when I need them
'How are you'
How long can you ask the same question?

All these dangers loom unless I go to Panskura
In Panskura
I don't ever lack for words
There are no problems.

I haven't been to the Santhal Parganas
Haven't been to Bankura
Haven't been to Murshidabad
That's probably why my life's been wasted

I stay here in Baranagar, in Calcutta
Everyone here wants their fortune read
They want to know what life holds for them
They want to know when they'll come into money

And I, an ancient ghost
Keep struggling on with imagery, symbol and resonance
To hell with day before yesterday's poems
All women with large breasts are better than them

Conjuring up thoughts about Panskura is better
Even writing four or five ordinary lines
About tender blades of grass is better

The Sheriff

Life has been going on this way
No one knows our sheriff's name

Who wrote *Red Oleanders*?
Who is the mainstay of our cricket team?
Who is our information and broadcasting minister?
Everyone supplies the names at once
But no one knows our sheriff's name

Do you?

To tell the truth, I haven't
Worried about our sheriff's identity either
Does he look after us with great care?
Does he read a lot at night?

Children will always scream
The children want to know: Who's the sheriff?

Can you let them know his name?

This Night-time, This Night

Let the night deepen, I'll speak then

Like whose hand does this night-time, this night,
Console me today
Forgetting complexities, people have fallen asleep. Only I
Am fiercely awake to see everything, to sense
This night-time, this night.
Where did you find
Such a block of darkness, night?
Those who are mute like me find release at night
Forgetting about extravagance
They draw life to themselves, try to live a little
I want to live some more too, want
Some money to myself
Mohan Singh saves me from every peril in a flash
Write, he tells me. I write. I
Write to you to me I write about Parul

The night—like a gigantic bird—floats away

Death

When death stands at the doorstep
What do you do?
What do all of you do?
Do you tremble?
Do you hand over the bank papers to your wife?
Do you ask for a glass of water?

The way I've seen life
The way I've thought it to be
Is pretty much how I've spent it

Plenty of mistakes
Persist
So many things I never got to say
Not nearly enough of laughter and stories

Trouble is really
Looming large over life now

What to do

Should I call my daughter to myself for a bit?

Living a few days more
Wouldn't have been bad

The Blue Planet

(1999)

Joy

Even after my death, I will write
Poetry and send it to all of you
All your life you will write one letter
After another to an extraordinary girl
And exchange blows.
And the wind will
Buffet your empty lives.
You know nothing at all of joy.
All morning I will
Write poetry. All afternoon I will
Write poetry. And all day long
A blue
Breeze will blow for me. And birds
Will come flying to me
With news of Calcutta

Not a Grenade

I shudder whenever I remember last winter
This time too the chill is quite twisted
Really, I'm going through such terrible days
Dulal's mother died the day before yesterday
Am I forgetting how to stay alive?

What is this country I have arrived at?
I can't quite tell
Shamsher is travelling in Europe without returning
  my eleven rupees
Buddhadeb is in Berlin or maybe Calcutta
—Sir, do you know the precise direction
Bangla poetry is moving in right now?

Despite thoughts of death it's true I'm alive
Where are Beethoven's letters?
I want to read those things once more
As for my old life, I want
To fold it and put it away in a suitcase. I can't even imagine
How calm and beautiful and sacred I become
When I come to you

Who Opened the Window

The woman who used to love me very much
Found her husband
Was bitten by a dog yesterday
She's very busy with the doctor and medicines now

Standing on a crowded road no longer
Enthrals me

From the dark cigarette shop I'm
Flying now
In the distance, there in the distance, Debu's wife is buying
 mustard

I'm happy, I'm forgetting everything

Calcutta

I really shall run away from this Calcutta one day
There's only the sound of breaking glass in Calcutta
The clang of knives and forks being flung on the floor
I shan't stay here
Here women knit all day and all night beneath a strange clock

Jibanananda Das: In Memoriam

When I think of him I don't send a telegram,
   only a light is switched on
And I see my heart as white as a flag of truce
I didn't sleep last night nor the night before but still there's
   no fatigue
I shan't go to work any more, I know, the light is not for me
It's been years since ordinary people have had ordinary bread
The police are here to investigate the theft almost a month later
Tramlines, tramlines, everyone is looking for him today
Wiping out suave banalities
Rinsing them off—a hundred years later the house he lived in
   will be nationalized.

Bones

The afternoon passes, I get blisters on my body. My bones
Lie on their back in the blast of heat
Perhaps they want to go back towards an illusory life

Seven mistakes buffet my head continuously

Next Monday
I don't want the bones to become the subject of conversation
  again

I'd prefer a sense of life
Which requests others to live

Even though the bones insist on remaining scattered

Forty

Today I saw morning reach afternoon,
Afternoon, evening,
And evening, night.

I remember the days before my birth

Are the leaves on the trees
Trying to say something on this suffocating night?

The prose writer returned home this instant, rapt in thought

How I've reached forty
Is something I must write a poem about tomorrow

Any

We eat up any news in two to ten minutes
We destroy anyone out of sheer whimsy
We snatch any city with a snap of our fingers
We choose to love any woman like a demon

The spring breeze still blows on time in spring
The sparrow is carrying a straw home in its beak
Whose daughter are you, bathed in pavement grime
We want peace we want peace peace is very wobbly

We sit in any hell with tethered hands and feet
We turn any sky to ashes with a finger-tilt
We sell any virgin by kilogrammes weighed on scales
OK let me say it: We like being somewhat crude

A Few Fragments of Love

1

It's drizzling tonight
I'm writing down the rain now

I'm not unhappy
That you didn't stay with me eventually

I understand the language of rain now
I understand the language of night
I can weep quietly in my own language now

2

Night is here to unfasten the wings of dreams again.
Listen. You consider yourself very pretty?
Go back to your husband if you like
I will go to an ugly girl somewhere
To cry in silence—may her loneliness,
Her clear-eyed joy, construct me
In the calm light of the night it seems
The world will one day be even more beautiful
Than I had imagined

About Women

1

'Women aren't like that'—having the last word calmly
My friend's friend went home.

I float, float away
Swimming without motion

Memories on my fingertips, memories in the rooms
Are awakened

Night is like that girl's serene hands

2

Cruelty? A very familiar word. Morning and evening
If it's survival here it's silence there

Abort? Very little. Aborted. In wombs
Girls are only aborted.

Still a girl like a virgin flower
Laughs somewhere

A slightly warm, indistinct light fills the earth.

The Window

Each of us is a bird of disbelief
Flapping our wings beneath the tired water
We shall be born, we *shall* be born, a new life
Tomorrow or the day after—maybe even this evening

° • •

The Blue Planet

1

Time is collapsing in space
The blue constellation is suspended constantly
I want relief from jiggling my knees in the second-floor room
At a meeting without a president
No one's willing to close the proceedings
I walk along, a Rs 2.80 book on my shoulder
Ancient notions are leaving us
Ancient poetry is leaving us
Taking a light shower in the evening
The earth is smiling gently

2

An eternal building
Stands by an eternal cloud

From the eternal sky
Eternal rain falls on Calcutta

Eternal girls
Are advancing towards eternal boys

Eternal, for ever
Ours

Ananyo Roy

With a light stroke of his fingers, blowing out in an instant
Brushing us aside with an arm
He jumped

Maybe the manager sahib
Took down what he said

The chair is empty now. Suddenly
An arrogant darkness has descended on the city

The hour of the furnace past,
Handing out opera tickets, he appears
To be gliding with a new green planet stuffed in his jacket

And will return in three or four days

A Piece of the Twenty-First Century

Seated in a chair without wheels
A gentleman
Was drifting between stars

Between cloud and clouds
His chair
Whistled past

In the morning he came down to earth
Soaped himself and bathed
Wrote a couple of letters seeking sexual friendship
And went to sleep

Irritation and more irritation
So much irritation on waking up
Seated in his chair
The gentleman filled his lungs with smoke

In the evening he voyaged to the stars again

Song

Bending his body slightly
The man who's dancing
And singing
Dressed in saffron
Is a baul.
What music is
Why music
Are things I have
Spoon-fed you
That song I spoke of . . . remember it?
Can you tell me the first line?
The second?
What a song! Oho!

How Are You, Humans?

(2005)

Come, Let's Talk of Some Things

Cut off this thing that has bothered you all your life

You are alive because of one simple reason, that you're inhaling and exhaling. Keep this task up.

Some more devastating storms are coming your way. Don't be nervous.

Don't assume that any night could be the last. Don't swallow a pill of indifference. Come, let's sit down and talk. Come, let's listen to music.

You must realize that the dark cannonballs being hurled at us have not been sent from the Middle Ages.

You will regain your lost youth right next to Shyamasree cinema.

Do you wish to remain near a world that's languishing? If your answer is yes, tick on the top right of the form. Enlist your name at our office.

Listen, don't be despondent.

The Giraffe

When a giraffe smeared with blood rises very late at night
Rises from language, shakes his head, and says:
Forget your toy household covered in ash
Drop your tears for fellow humans
Your tears for the world
All you have loved are fat deposits, violence
Tonight the heart wants just the smell of cottonwool and Dettol
There's no hope of real cottonwool and Dettol, I gave it up
   long ago
I too am not allowed to talk or to smoke
A famous doctor has said I'll survive
All I think is, I'll survive, I'll survive
When a giraffe smeared with blood rises very late at night

Yes and No

First I write a single yes. Then I scratch it out.
After this I write no. No.
Now I feel lighter. I look for tea.
A tune or two gather in my throat.
A face floats up. From thirty years ago.
Yes, that face from sixty-seven. Nineteen sixty-seven.
So much failure in my life, I muse. Such futility. Still
That face is an achievement. A joy. Some rest.

I just wrote joy.
I just wrote rest.
I simply cannot scratch the words out any more. I feel sleepy.
I sleep.

Between Love and Unlove

Between love and unlove lurk one or two cats.
They wag their tails. Some days
I scurry about busily. Some days, I keep sitting.
I'm getting by with small talk and tomatoes and spinach.
I break into laughter.
And then suddenly a wailing cancels everything out
Refusing to let me talk.
If a jeep were available, I might have left the gathering and run
Or put a slim volume on the table and said: Read this, then.
None of this happens, the days pass in drudgery alone
   in a room
The days pass and the people nearby
Drift away like ghosts
Colliding, the evenings break down, become twisted
Sleep embraces me like a fat, dark woman

An Incident

The clock rang two. Then three. And nothing happened.
Children in different colours started going home from school.
The sun rolled on, slumping on the western horizon
Only, when night deepened
The man smashed his fist into the window
Sprinkling the room with shards of glass, and blood

Who Isn't Talented, After All?

You won't have to dazzle too much. Or talk too much. Stay ordinary, like a braid of hair. Like an uneventful afternoon. Slack. Scattered.

I want you to organize your discarded thoughts. Don't step on the staircase on which the blind man is winding his way upwards. Here people shrivel up like a strand of rope and die. Call them.

Open up a garden of butterflies amid the ogres, and look, they're turning into humans. Was Agastya a poet? Don't waste away in unhappiness and extravagance. Eat fruit every afternoon.

As for the man who keeps praising you every morning and evening, tell him with a smile that you know him through and through.

About the Afternoon

You can never write enough about the afternoon. These afternoons are a lot like empty drinking dens during the day. Just stillness. Only silence.

Do you understand just what this thing called silence is?

In the distance a man is chasing sparrows away from the window. And I am writing down all this, silent, ragged, in a notebook.

A shadow-laden wind just entered the room. And vanished into the horizon.

The afternoon—all right, I'll say it—is like Mrs Chaturvedi. Just keeps me sitting face to face in silence.

Chant

Ceaselessly the sun rises and sets
Day one moment, night the next
I cannot keep pace any more

And who are you come straight into my room?
It's true I've seen you once or twice
Are you not going to say: I'm your wife?

There's something I chant quite often nowadays
Don't cover yourself up
If you wish, wander around and laugh and die
Don't go looking for love like a detective

A Winter Night

A winter
Midnight
Someone
Said something
The words were lost
In sleep

Take Care of Yourself

How to keep your eyes healthy and shining
Have you read the article?
Seen the cutting-edge ad about reviving sexuality?
What do you read all day anyway?
Ruins? Gautam's story? *The Journal*?
And really, how much poetry can you read
And how much will you dance with a light the colour of darkness?
Think a little about wellness now
'Lust causes death'. The sentence caught my eye one day
    while leafing through the Bible
Simplify your lifestyle now—watch theatre, visit Kenduli for a
    concert of baul music
What I'm saying is, relax, relax a bit now

Scratches

On black ink
Tragic scratches of red
It's nothing.
It really is nothing
Unless you recollect
A boy with black skin
Bloodied
Asleep for ever in the rice field

Letting Go

If my work is done
Let me go

All morning and afternoon and evening
All alone

The shops are brightly lit all year
What are you buying—shoe polish or deodorant?
Or soap, every day?

A golden moss has encircled me
Let me go

Life

There's no sense in wasting life
No sense at all
There's no sense in cutting life short
No sense at all
If people can laugh even when sleeping on a winter pavement,
What's your problem
What's your problem
The slightest darkness makes you pant twenty-four hours a day
Makes you pant

That's quite something

Earth

Everyone's got a nuclear bomb
As soon as the button is pressed, any time at all,
Twelve or thirteen earths will explode
What fun, there's only one earth
Like a lemon swinging
At the end of a string
In space

Human

The way a human burns alive
Is not how a corpse burns on a pyre
Silence has prevailed for an hour or two
Across the river in the afternoon
Still a fire rages somewhere
Something still burns—must be a human

Sir

Impossible. Writing anything about
Him is impossible.
He's
One in a million.
I know
I am a poet of a decade. He,
Of the millennium.

To Debarati

Never mind letters
I don't even care to ring anyone on the phone any more

I was supposed to send you something by the post
I didn't forget but things have become difficult
Every time I climb upstairs I gasp for breath
Stuffing not one but two inhalers into my mouth

A confusing time of turmoil all around
It's not as though the nose stud is dazzling
Two faces probably snagged on either side of the poison sac

I'm reading your new book

I don't know how to tell you
How wonderful your poetry is, Debarati

Anxiety

No more letters.
Calcutta does all its talking on the phone.
Do you wish you could
Sit face to face with people and speak?
Throw your old-fashioned demands into the river
Swallow them
Wind up your home

My feet are stuck to the city, befuddled
Inside my head
Someone has lit a candle.
I wonder why I still prefer balloons to flowers
Why do people seem taller
Than skyscrapers and shorter than even rats
Come let's huddle together to live
With our arms around one another
Else we'll erupt we'll be shattered into fragments
Into fragments

One more delicate separation
Another sharp-edged loneliness is almost here
With a grain or two of sugar in their mouths
Each has just retreated into its hole

Some people have courteously and deftly set aside
Our existence—I haven't seen
The angry young man in a long time
The boy who used to sing on his way back has long disappeared
You want to hear him again? You want to see him again?
Stroking my cheek, the past left for Behrampore yesterday
The present is bubbling up in a monstrous froth of smoke
We're getting by with our coughs and colds
What about you?

Time is short and what are you muttering in half-sleep?

But then what's there to say anyway
If only the bed wouldn't wait till 3 a.m. to welcome me
Sleep, like an epic, has taken its leave
Civilization sits with one hand on suicidal inclinations
At night in Salt Lake the car
Keeps going round in circles

Unbuttoning their clothes, the women are sunk in long slumber
Half the people in the country are thought-leaders
Delivering speeches with their eyes closed in such deep emotion
What are you staring at in wonder from the pavement, Santosh
Go home
Note down all the things that have come to pass
Viewing the world over the rims of their glasses
They're all climbing up the stairway to heaven.
Although it's not written in the scriptures or anywhere in India
We're dragging ourselves on our bellies towards death

We'll die from a shortage of homes and of food
Lacking friends despite travelling through seven heavens
Lacking love despite travelling through seven hells
Convicted of the crime of talking to ourselves
And of the crime of sleeping by ourselves
Like a cat spreadeagled on the street
We will have to languish, flattened.

I don't know when it began
This complex and more complex game
And it's not as though it will end because it has begun
Let's go take a look
Whether the earth is turning, whether it's still turning
Only the half-mad get electric shocks and turn fully mad here
They sneer at each other, sandpaper one another's mouths
We put some of our annoyances aside as we we drink our
    afternoon tea
Are we nightmares? Or burnt-down trees?
Why does the royal ghost of extravagance still attract me?
Amid all this strife and trouble, Sumit, let me tell you
We must survive, we must survive
This time in Santiniketan
Our wonderment, sensation of pain, and love were awakened
Our insignificant dreams came back
We missed being introduced to the beautiful woman by
    a heartbeat
What shall we do? What can we do? What is there to do?
Shall we look around on the assumption that the world is
    shrouded by god?

And, concluding that everything will end well, shall we
Do a little dance?
So many ships were launched to the sound of conchshells
and ululation
A thousand benedictions were pronounced
So much progress, so much romance
So many wedding vows to the strains of the shehnai, and
Violent partings, with swearwords on the side, the very next
moment
A procession passed with flags held aloft, chanting 'Fight to live'
I wonder who pushed away my poetry from the smooth surface
of the table
Did life become precarious?
Nothing like that—all day and night
Like a coarse brushmark, futile, failed time marches on
Behind all these roads and cars and crowds of people
The anxious face that keeps peeping out at regular intervals
Is, as everyone has guessed today, mine.

Beautiful

It's true I'm somewhat bewildered
Some ugly illnesses have arrived too, entwined together
Some who were friends all this while
Who sang, who kept time to music
Giant craftsmen of language, part policemen . . .
I'm still aware of some of their fine art

Silence is a weapon with which, you must know, people can be
    made to disappear

I survived because of the shadows and winding lanes
Everyday faces, slim books, which are my gratitude
Of course, when the brown dogs appear
With their puppies to rub their noses on my knee for biscuits
I only reflect how I've wasted the days
It seems nothing is more beautiful than being alive

The Epitaph

You trees, leaves on trees
All you silent stars in the sky
Space and time
All living creatures
Water, river water, listen
I was here
My head was a butterfly
Flying a million light years,
A city ghost, I was born in the city
And it was here I died and rotted

The Language of Giraffes

(2005)

1

Finally all wishes have vanished
Dreams lie scattered on their faces
What can you do
You madman
Besides writing, and persistently writing, all day and night

2

Now to live like a ghost in the room
How distant one life is from another
No words, even the songs have left with a laugh
Like a bat, all the time
My days end with the thought 'We don't belong to each other'

3

They want to see me flailing as I die
Dying, I'm just dying. They want to see
Me wandering in the jungle alone—on city roads
Walking naked, hanging from a noose
It's true that I am dying. But partly by choice, partly without.

4

I want to see the final truth in this lie-encircled world
The violence that burns me every day
The cruelty to which I lose every time
A society of nerveless light
In which I want to sense the call of Om. This, just this.

5

Two or three lines of sweat trickled down my neck at night
On the crest of a wave I rose and fell
The burning days came back to say: cleanse us
And accept us
I may have asked for too much—life has passed without peace

6

I was walking in space on my way back
My adolescence was meaningless
My youth was awkward, vacuous
How could I have seen such poison during my days
Is there still something called life? It's ashes, just ashes

7

My life has passed caged in long sleep
On this declining night in Bengal I confess
Death has troubled me a great deal
Life has annoyed me too, still,
There was something—human existence, perhaps, or your face
   of rain

8

Those who have survived are strolling on the evening street
How do you live, my heart, to the sound of falling, of slipping?
Life has long been poisoned
In this city of commerce
I must burn night and day—but I alone will have to die

9

Be calm, you with the auspicious name, listen,
Even if your sorrows do not leave you, will you
Leap from the roof or take a hundred sleeping pills?
How can you? What sort of heart do you have? Waves
Rise, and fall again, let's try more, let's live, let us live

10

If I can return after traversing this darkness
I'll speak
Forgive me, forgive me today, my lovely
I must shake off the darkness in my face in my heart in my head
Like a middle-aged woman. That's all the afternoon is saying

11

I didn't bathe today—lunch at a dhaba on B. T. Road
My wife's at a meeting, she'll be late.
I'm looking for you, what if you were also looking for me?
I obey the orders of a meaningless life
Poetry, poetry, a life of just poetry is pure madness

12

What a morning it was, with no protective wear
I have no problem whatsoever with my talent
I only wonder why I've never met Anjana Bhowmick
Some people have smashed everything with hockey sticks
The body sank long ago—only the head is floating

13

Think of the stormy nights you've had to live through
You've seen many trains go past the city at night
There was once a coming home in the dark, a wasted childhood
My life is a shriek of pain
Concealed beneath conversations, songs and girls' laughter

14

Of course there was melancholy but I didn't let it have its head
Blood, anxieties, despair sought me out every day
How long can one go on sleeping and waking without reason?
My head was a green magic
I'm off with a cup of coffee to wipe out sadness

15

For sometime now I'm entangled with it's nothing
A constant annoyance has laid siege from nowhere
This freak reluctance with a hundred feet is irking me the most
Why must I tolerate all this?
You came long ago, loneliness, why can't you leave now?

16

No way forward now darkness screams darkness love
I'm exhausted and out of words and steamrolled
In the darkness I sit talking to the darkness
What does it mean to be alive? Is this how man lives, alone,
Reading in a cell, writing letters, panting, dying suddenly?

17

The day snaps shut like a lid on a snake, I'm startled
When will I shed all this rage and weariness, thinker?
Time's running out—the evening cloud today
Has a crimson glow
Only one way, my friend, work all day, wash your hands, bathe

18

I've laid out very little flesh for the soul
I have walked to the sleepless zone today
It's not just talk: I must escape
This loneliness, this circle of poison
Will you give me ten minutes from your life?

19

The wind swirls and slams into the room
Pages of unread books fly up to the bed
Crossing a road or two, have you ever visited this room?
My days too are coming to an end
Whenever I'm reminded of death, I want to light a cigarette

20

It's evening, the fever's 102, sleep calls, eyes close
It feels like a procession around me with torches
Have I been born on earth after death?
Why am I so bereft of words?
Why can't I flail my limbs and talk of living?

21

Just how does the world feel in 2000? A room stuffed
  with rainbows?
A flying horse? A tree with wings?
I had been burnt to death by a purple ambition
Still, I'm fine
Lips move and none of us can hear one another

22

I understand all my madness and babble now
Would it have been very difficult to switch on a light and sink into
  the newspaper at night?
This being alive—what is this being alive?
Like a soliloquy of gibberish
I languish, close to the eddies of life and eddies of death

23

This night and this darkness and you face to face with them, alone
A quiet breeze and someone's fallen asleep with the radio on
Are you enjoying the life that you've got?

Is it painful? Is it lonely? Far too lonely?
Wherever there's a footprint I see blood appearing

24

'How smart your violence is,' I say and come downstairs
To find the wind blowing and buses winging over the city
We just claw at one another
Putting this one on a pedestal, flinging that one to dust
I am dumb like a corroded dream. Let's go, cry the buses

25

Death, to tell you the truth, isn't in my thoughts now
There was a time of suffering for leaving the world
Like a little boy I would once be in agony
Because I would have to abandon life
The night is the poets' friend, you are my mother, night

26

I gaze helplessly at a collapsed land
Tomorrow's and tomorrow's clouds have darkened
Who are these dancing in our country?
Have we lost all our words?
That girl's face is lovelier much lovelier than the rose

27

Is the cavorting subconscious saying, 'We're primitive'?
That we're dressed as clowns to stave off relief?

Women attain freedom, become prettier perhaps
The temple and the mosque collided hard
Just the other day, I saw some of it on TV

28

I see my innocent soul's been sold for seventeen rupees
Will I no longer be spotted on the streets then?
Am I a nightmare in that case? Lacking respect?
Why is the blood dripping?
God knows Allah knows how high the fever is

29

Still I have to stand in the blackness and see
Still I must see the gaudiness of the idiot's false teeth and smiles
Floating in the darkness I see
The sudden light of the light
The world charmed by people charmed by itself is joy itself

30

Don't weep and cry, 'Save me,' young man
Come let me make you famous in two hours
Go home with a smile, with guile
Be renowned and go home
You write beautifully, what more do you want in life, handsome?

31

'The evening is young.' The women dining at the table
Frowned at me, like a storm of fire

Swimming and swallowing the water of hell
I was on my way too
With a dream like a perennial spring and a couple of manuscripts

32

Gulping down a volcano like smoke I lie on my belly
So many clashes between you and me and a thousand songs
To cut through it a path an inch deep, we must walk on sand
—Whose painting is that? Rousseau's or Chagall's?
   Maybe Dali's?
Who follows art these days, when thousand turn to portraits
   in a flash

33

Still the shadows walk and talk, some of them fall asleep
Still the game might start, a rousing rhythm
Some left, some rushed in gasping
Collapsing on chairs
Racing about on the streets—an unseeing day, the stench returns

34

How do we accomplish so much with just two hands at our
   disposal
Look, see for yourself, what a celebration of buttocks, songs
So many fountains of light and
Girls holding candles at inaugurations, prawns and lobsters
Here it's an icy evening, the children wandering, their home's
   vanished

35

I'm sure I saw you first in a mountain land, beautiful woman
Was it covered only by mist, and winter rain and frost?
You were in a skirt in June of 1961
What splendid beauty what a gift you held in your breast
Today there's only a silence and the reverberation of two
    or three silences

36

Did I then choose on my own to move so far away?
It's true that blood isn't all that flows from the mouth
Lesions can't be seen, the losses are mute children of indifference
Everything else about us is normal
The trees, green, and the sky a tranquil blue, the faces pale

37

'My prayer was to live like many-hued Nadia District'
A man was telling a gentle woman
A dark night or two, a dark wind or two of silence
Had said while whirling in my room:
Poetry is a forlorn girl in a skirt—hear her, be near her

38

Come to terms with the days that are here, cohabit with them
What are these days and nights for, human? All these days
    and nights?
Flames are falling from the sky just as many flames in the air
Dance, corpse-clearing woman, dance, in this demoness time

In the blood of our mothers and fathers we're streams of
  blood today

39

When all the terrible humiliation nudges life mildly
When an unprotected existence turns weary
When time appears to demand, do something, sir,
I plunge into the darkness
Whatever I fling away, thinking it's a bomb, turns into a flare

40

How will I write again without innumerable mornings in my life
Unless I see the geese flying in from the east to land
Or the swaying and sprouting of the china rose
How will there be poetry, thoughts of poetry
With nothing to say and trite smiles, I really am still an imbecile

41

Someone said you've left the capital suddenly for Barcelona
The word 'Barcelona' makes me think of a piano at once
Who's playing it? Who's listening, for that matter?
Magical sunlight in this solitude, sunglasses,
You walk alone on the pavement, I follow close behind you

42

Why have you wrapped your time around your blood your nerves?
What had to be has been already, what will be, will be

We had plenty of evidence too, living
Things that we wrote, still, words wander
We have no language no rhythm we're just water chestnuts

43

I'll leave Calcutta now for another, quieter, Calcutta
What do you think, Mrs Bhandarkar?
Listen to me, Pandit-ji will sing there mornings and evenings
I'll find so many things to talk about with a smile
Say what you will, life's an annoyance, though it says, stay,
    just stay

44

I saw a lovely girl in the city of Calcutta today
So very beautiful, how can I describe her
It's true, young man, we're alive for the sake of love
All agony abates one day like agony abates
I'll probably forget the lovely girl from lovely Calcutta
    in a day or two

45

Was the world ever so intolerant, bad-tempered, adamant?
There's a fire I will burn in, I have set aside some of it
In the pages of a book
I must go to Colootola to gauge the mood of a fat committee
The world will not change the way you expect it to

46

Next week you'll know, you'll realize, what poverty is
You became an important man
You thought penury would never reach you again
A tongue like fire, a paw like a policemen
The poison sac is ripped it's openly two-faced now

47

On these ordinary days near mercury and gunpowder
How are you, mankind?
Are you just like me? As lonely as a dog's yellow vomit?
Calcutta is certain to forget me now
Still I think, a good morning will beckon, come over,
    Purulia will say

48

Leaving these octaves behind, I feel like sitting near you
    for two hours
My third eye is lost
I haven't seen the face of the one coming up the stairs today
It isn't my life's philosophy to bring you grief
I'm going away because one has to, or I'd have stayed a while
    longer

Unpublished and Uncollected Poems

Seven or Eight Hundred Kilometres

A road seven or eight hundred kilometres long
The inevitable scene of a speeding car
A suspended bridge emerging from a river after a dip
A sharp knife soaked in three hundred years of blood
—'I love you, Nancy'—'I love you too, Peter'
I was looking for peanuts looking for my girlfriend

Death has no sense of timing. Comes whenever it likes.

The Language of Giraffes

1

How swiftly the years race away
At dusk a face or two floats up
My friends are resting
Far away
In my life only leaves are shed

2

My existence is a hospital
So I've often thought in the noonday sun
In the after-afternoon, when life
Is drowsy
No one, nothing, seems to exist, near and far

3

Because you'll come, I've snagged a wicker chair
I wonder, will you come? Will you really come?
Two decades have passed—or four? I still sit in the darkness
Why this loneliness, why this pulse in my veins
You are mild (fragrant air), peace, peace in my nerves,
    panacea

Time, My Time

Once again
In the galaxy
A new planet has been discovered

All of us
Sit smiling
Charmed by the imported soap we're holding

The children are playing

Who'd guess that so many wars
Are leaning over my shoulder

About His Death

It's not as though he was the only one to die at 8 am
It was a Saturday
My younger sister had died at 8 a.m. too
The next Saturday Shamsher died at 5 past 8
Dipak Mujumdar? No, he bid goodbye in the afternoon
I was wandering
Shamsher was in a coma a full 4 months
Who knows how many sleeping pills he had taken
I had entered Shamsher's cabin but hadn't quite recognized him
The regal form had vanished and there was a smell in the room
Which was quite suspicious
We'd have both gained from a conversation
At 20 I had told Shamsher I'd write till 55
Who knows why I had said 55
Who knows why I keep writing of death and about death
Ridiculous thing to do
Isn't there anything in life besides death?

Swimming

It was raining in Rameshwar
Taking photos was impossible

This was a favourite thrill
Our car would drive
Over the Second Hooghly Bridge
Into the city

Tikia, rumali roti
It's by your grace that I survive
That I survive
I swim

In the city's belly, and

At your window, beautiful woman

Rocket

We live beneath the same roof
Sometimes there's rain and sometimes fog
Come, my rocket, just keep on flying
We are lost and again we return

. • .

Conjugality 2

Did you ever know
There were so many clouds within clouds?

Tomorrow
We might go our separate ways

But today?
On this quiet, still evening

Come, let's listen to music

While Everyone's Asleep at Night . . .

While everyone's asleep at night the girl's writing me a letter
I'm not the kind of person who remembers spelling mistakes
I have travelled a thousand miles to find
The light from her face falling on mine
Her garden, her casuarinas, her little house
Have merged into my life and my tiny room
A gossamer dream is approaching us ever so quietly

A Brown Poem

What use would it be if you came back today
Daylight's passed, suddenly the lamp's gone out

The winter sun was a blanket, that's true
In the times of restaurants
It seems like an infatuation now

What use would it be if you lit the lamp
I've forgotten everything
I might not even recognize you

Through the Window

My body is still numb—all day long I hear
The pounding of blood
Medicines, doctor, only needles in my veins
Don't listen to film songs, don't, look,
Schoolboys and
Schoolgirls pass, happy, rapt, dreams on their faces

Advice

—Wind the clock at eight or nine
—And then?
—And then listen to the radio
—And then?
—And then go to office
—And then?
—And then be a tiny bird
And fly into the sky
Keep flying

Nicotine

I seek you all night my life breaks in a flash
You are flowing in my blood
You cannot sweep me away, but still I know
I cannot live without you without your fragrance

One Day of Love at Nineteen or Twenty

I'd gifted you four plastic flowers
Whom did you give them to?
I'd saved the cloudy days in my pocket
Where have those days gone, hmm?
Don't you have any shame at all?
Go tell your mother I want a cup of coffee now
Whatever has to happen should happen this evening
Where's your father? Your brothers and sisters?

Dawn

The night is deeper now
Your face is even closer to mine
I have an urge
To walk a long way along the empty streets
Someone must have switched off all of Calcutta's lights
Only a lamp burns in my room
I can see your face
I can hear your breath
It's almost dawn

A Few Lines

1

Never go near your friends
Be alone as long as you can
Never go near your lover
Be alone as long as you can

2

All gone, yet
Only a heart can
Still go near a heart

Blood

Blood oozes out in drops, constantly
The blood of a moment
Drips on another
 . . . Cleaning my glasses, I read history
Blood oozes out in drops
On the bed
Blood drips along my entire life

The House

(To Debarati Mitra)

The yellow gate is opened
The house sleeps, only
The desk and chair remain awake

The house sleeps every day
Falls asleep in the morning, falls asleep in the evening
It sleeps so soundly at night—storms rage, rains come
From a distance you can see
The trees calling
The house wildly

The house sleeps, refuses to wake up

Two Poems

1

Have you become an eagle? I don't see you any more, the sun rises
Clouds—they float away too every day
The blue light that burns over Calcutta's head
Every evening
Keeps burning—but I don't see you. Have you left our land
Leaping over mountains?
Lying diagonally on the bed
I too get out of bed with the thought of going far away
Only to lie down again—early on Saturdays I put
A cigar in my mouth, it burns
All the lost stories come back one by one, I go back

From the bed in the evening I hear the distant weeping of
    mermaids
Rising from the water far away
So much smoke everywhere, I feel you may be
Hidden in the smoke
But actually there's no one, the stars in the sky sink into the earth
All the lice in my hair die
Are you dead too? I don't see you any more, the sun rises
Clouds—they float away too every day

The blue light that burns over Calcutta's head
Every evening
Keeps burning—but I don't see you. Have you become an
   eagle?

2

The sun touches the old school building, doesn't touch me

In My Sleep

Rainfall in my sleep, two inches of water in my chest cavity
Only indistinctness and love
Sit across the river all the time——the red dust of Jhumritila
Is still embedded in my nails
The sound of hooves fades in the distance, returns in my heart
As though I will die
Of a lack of sorrow——water in my chest cavity, rainfall, seven
    million
Hairs left behind on my bed

Notes

Cheiro: William John Warner (1866–1936). Irish astrologer and occult figure of the early twentieth century. His sobriquet, Cheiro, derives from the word *cheiromancy*, meaning palmistry. A self-proclaimed clairvoyant, he taught palmistry, astrology and Chaldean numerology.

Keo Karpin oil: Very popular brand of hair oil produced, since 1956, in West Bengal by the renowned Dey's Medical Group of Companies.

Hooghly District: Located in southern West Bengal, about 40 km from Calcutta. Remained under indigenous rulers until the thirteenth century when the Portuguese, the Dutch, the French, the Danes and the English settled here and utilized it as their point of entry to the rest of India.

The Giuoco Piano: The Giuoco Piano is a chess opening beginning with the moves:

    1. e4 e5
    2. Nf3 Nc6
    3. Bc4 Bc5

White's 'Italian bishop' at c4 prevents Black from advancing to the centre with d5 and attacks the vulnerable f7 square. White plans to dominate the center with d2–d4 and to attack the Black king. Black aims to free his game by exchanging pieces and playing the pawn break d5, or to hold his centre pawn at e5. One of the oldest recorded openings. The Portuguese Damiano played it at the beginning of the sixteenth century and the Italian Greco played it at the beginning of the seventeenth. Also known as the Italian Game. Popular through the nineteenth century, but modern refinements in defensive play have led most chess masters towards other openings that offer White greater chances for long-term initiative.

Page 47

Dehra Dun: The capital city of Uttarakhand in North India. Located in the Garhwal region, in the foothills of the Himalayas and between two of India's mightiest rivers—the Ganges on the east and the Yamuna on the west. Famous for its picturesque landscape and mild climate.

Page 49

Shrabon: Fourth month of the Bengali Hindu calendar, and usually the second month of the monsoons in eastern India.

Page 52

Baroda: Vadodara. City in Gujarat, on the banks of the Vishwamitri river, southeast of Ahmedabad, 139 km from the state capital Gandhinagar. Site of the Lakshmi Vilas Palace, residence of the Maharaja of Baroda and the royal family. Also home to the Maharaja Sayajirao University, the largest university in the state.

Barisha: Residential locality of Calcutta. One of the oldest boroughs. Abode of the great Sabarna Roy Choudhury family. One of the major educational and cultural hubs of the metropolis.

Jadavpur: Southern neighbourhood of Calcutta. Location of some of India's major learning institutes, including the Jadavpur University, the Indian Association for the Cultivation of Science and the Indian Institute of Chemical Biology. To accommodate the sudden post-Independence increase in population (from East Bengal, now Bangladesh), a large number of colonies emerged in some areas of Calcutta. Jadavpur was one such area.

Bethuadahari: Located in the Nadia District of West Bengal. Famous for its wildlife sanctuary.

Page 65

B. T. Road: Barrackpore Trunk Road, part of West Bengal State Highway 1, connecting Shyambazar in North Calcutta to Barrackpore, a military and administrative centre under British rule and the scene of several acts of rebellion against the British during the nineteenth century. The oldest cantonment in India.

Page 74

Malkosh: Also known as Malkaus/h. One of the oldest ragas of Indian classical music. The name is derived from the combination of *Mal* and *Kaushik*, which means 'he who wears serpents like garlands'—the god Shiva. Meant for the late night.

Page 90

Panskura: City and municipality in Purba Medinipur District of West Bengal.

Santhal Parganas: Areas inhabited by the Santhals, one of the largest indigenous tribes of India. One of the five administrative units of Jharkhand in eastern India. Created as a district of the Bengal Presidency in 1855.

Bankura: One of the seven districts of Burdwan Division in West Bengal. Described as the link between the plains of Bengal on the east and Chota Nagpur Plateau on the west. Centre of the historic Mallabhum (Malla Kingdom) of western Bengal. Vaishnavism, which gained the status of state religion in the Malla Kingdom in the seventeenth century, shaped the culture of the region. The Malla Kingdom was annexed by the British East India Company in 1765 and the modern Bankura District took its form in 1881 and was named after its headquarters.

Murshidabad: District of West Bengal. Murshidabad city, which lends its name to the district, was the seat of power of the nawabs of Bengal.

Baranagar: A municipality in Calcutta. Home to the Indian Statistical Institute. Also a major industrial centre.

Page 92

Red Oleanders: A play by Rabindranath Tagore, published in 1925, on the themes of unscrupulous capitalism, environmental exploitation and the importance of human relationships.

Page 101

Jibanananda Das (1899–1954): Considered one of the innovators who introduced modernist poetry to Bengali literature at a period when it was influenced by Rabindranath Tagore's Romantic poetry. According to critic Chidananda Dasgupta, 'While he is best known for poetry that reveals a deep love of nature and rural landscapes, tradition and history, Jibanananda is also strikingly urban, and introspective, his work centring on themes of loneliness, depression and death. He was a master of word-images, and his unique poetic idiom drew on tradition but was startlingly new.' Das died on 22 October 1954, eight days after he was hit by a tramcar.

Page 111

baul: Member of an order of religious singers of Bengal known for their unconventional behaviour and for the freedom and spontaneity of their mystical verse. Their membership consists both of Hindus (primarily Vaishnavites) and Muslims (generally Sufis). Their songs frequently deal with the love between the human personality and a personal god who resides within the individual. Little is known of the development of the cult, as their songs began to be collected and written down only in the twentieth century. Tagore was one of many Bengali authors who acknowledged his indebtedness of inspiration to baul verse.

Page 124

Kenduli: Village in the Bolpur subdivision of Birbhum District. Birthplace of the famous poet Jayadeva, and home to the annual festival of bauls.

Page 133

Behrampore: Administrative headquarters of Murshidabad District.

Salt Lake: Popular name of Bidhannagar, a satellite town of Calcutta. Developed between 1958 and 1965, and named after Dr Bidhan Chandra Roy, then chief minister of West Bengal. Built on a reclaimed salt-water lake.

Page 134

Santiniketan: A small town near Bolpur in Birbhum District of West Bengal; home to the Visva-Bharati University founded by Rabindranath Tagore.

Page 143

dhaba: Roadside restaurants, usually situated on highways and serving local cuisine.

Page 150

Nadia District: Situated in the heart of the Bengal delta with the Bhagirathi river in the west and the Mathabhanga river in the north. Takes its name from Nabadwip, birthplace of the fifteenth-century Hindu saint Shri Chaitanya Mahaprabhu.

Page 152

Colootola: Street in Central Calcutta, famous for its roadside bookstores.

Page 153

Purulia: One of the ancient kingdoms of North India. Now a district in West Bengal. Famous for the traditional dance form Chhau.

Page 161

Rameshwar: Rameswaram. Town in Ramanathapuram District of Tamil Nadu. Located on Pamban Island and separated from mainland India by the Pamban Channel. Together with Varanasi, it is considered to be one of the holiest places in India to Hindus. According to legend, the place from where Rama built a bridge across the sea to Lanka to rescue Sita from her abductor Ravana.

tikia: Indian fried patty of spiced meat or mashed potato.

rumali roti: Thin flatbread popular in India and Pakistan. Named after the rumal or handkerchief.

Page 176

Jhumritila: Also known as Jhumri Telaiya. Town in Koderma District of Jharkhand, India. Situated in the Damodar Valley.